TOWARD THE GLIMMER

Stories and Essays from the Korongo Writers Group

THERESA BRYANT   JOSIE CAROTHERS

PAM CORCORAN   LYDIA ENGLISH

JOAN FEIERABEND   PAT MENCHINI

LINDA MORSE   NANCY REID   NANCY TUCKER

———

For Sara Tucker, our mentor and friend. As we grow as writers, our thankfulness for her presence in our lives increases.

———

The Korongo Writers Group

———

We are a group of ten women writers from Central Vermont who are struggling to become stronger, clearer writers and, at the same time, follow a journey of self-discovery "toward the glimmer."

———

Contents

Nancy Reid

Nancy Tucker

TOWARD THE GLIMMER

Theresa Bryant

Running Toward Virtue
The Master Fixer and His Apprentice

For more than forty years, she had the good fortune to work in centers of learning, where words and language were essential to mission and message. Dubbing herself a professional communicator, she supported others to write, polish, frame, position their thoughts and voices to reach their intended audiences. The hats she donned and sites were varied: as editorial assistant to a gaggle of multicultural scholars in the department of psychiatry at the University of Hawaii at Manoa, marketing copywriter in continuing education at The Johns Hopkins University, presidential assistant to three college presidents at Western Maryland College, and College of Notre Dame in Maryland, and later as Vice President for Public Affairs (DePauw University) and Director of Alumni Relations (Dartmouth Medical School). The role from which she gleaned the greatest satisfaction was her first: as a high school English teacher.

Running Toward Virtue
THERESA BRYANT

I t was nearly 9 P.M. Hannah sat still as a huge boulder. Her eyes stared straight ahead at a fixed spot on the wall over the left shoulder of her social worker, seated behind a desk.

Meg Parson leaned forward toward the silent, immobile child. Since it was only Monday, the case files piled on her desk were still in relatively tidy order. Only one was opened—the one she was reviewing as she waited for a call from the precinct officer on duty.

In the room two voices, like strident strings scraping against each other, veered for dominance. At first the voice of Mother Wilson, Hannah's foster mother, blared forth. Then Meg Parson chimed back in clearer resonance. The point-counterpoint, back and forth, statements and questions, the two voices played against each other with momentary breaks meant for a response or refrain.

STATEMENT: "You're a good girl, Hannah. You never cause trouble in school or at home."

QUESTION: "Why are you doing this? Haven't I been good to you?"

Silence. No response.

QUESTION from Mother Wilson: "Why was she brought here? Why wasn't she taken home? Did you think I'd punish you?"

COUNTERSTATEMENT from Ms. Parson: "Hannah and Nate both have said kind things about you. And I get good reports from their school about the children too."

For a while, Hannah mumbled, "No ma'am" or "Yes, ma'am" at the proper question or lull for a response. But she began to lose her rhythm in the litany. So she stopped. She dropped her gaze to her lap.

Mother Wilson rose from her chair. Hannah felt her standing next to her. Her foster mother cupped her hand gently under her chin.

"You're not listening, are you, Hannah?"

She heard the voice and question. "I am," she said firmly. Though her chin had been lifted, her fixed gaze traveled slightly higher but not into the eyes above her.

"So what are we to do, young lady?"

Hannah offered no other response.

"Mrs. Wilson, why don't you have a seat now."

Hannah's jaw and shoulders had tightened at Mrs. Wilson's sudden touch.

"I think we've reached an impasse here, don't you?" Meg stood and gestured toward the chair Mrs. Wilson had occupied.

Hannah said quietly but loud enough for both women to hear, "I am not going back there." She raised her head and moved her face to lock eyes for just a moment with each of them. "I can't stay good in that house." Her voice trembled as she lowered her eyes again. "It's almost too late already," she uttered more quietly.

Mother Wilson stood again. Her voice was now

nervous and agitated. "What do you mean? What have you said to Ms. Parson?"

Hannah spoke without any prompting. "Her son is a bad person. He's mean to Nathan because he tries to protect me. He tries to make me do things that aren't nice." She had remained calm for as long as she could. She raised her hands to her face and softly moaned as if in pain.

Mother Wilson shouted, pivoting her raised hand between the wounded child and the listening social worker. "Well, I can't believe that Perry Junior would do anything to hurt Hannah." Turning again to Hannah, "Why, he's your big brother!"

"He's not my brother. Ask Nathan. He's seen him come at me." Hannah hoped no further explanation was necessary. How could Ms. Parson send her back?

Meg Parson stood and walked toward the door. "Mrs. Wilson, may we talk outside, please?" It was more a statement than a request. Mother Wilson hesitated, then exited ahead of her. Hannah could hear the conversation begin again outside the door.

"But she's the oldest girl. Who's going to help me with the housework? What about her school? Are you going to take Nathan, too?" Her foster mother's questions were louder than Ms. Parson's responses. The last question hung heavy in Hannah's ears.

Her brother Nate. What was going to happen to him? Hannah had taken Nate with her at least three other times when she ran away, but two children rarely escaped notice for very long, especially when they looked so much alike. This time, however, the plan had been to leave from school. Nate had been on board, but she would slip away on her own. "Don't take a beating over this," she had told him, "but cross your fingers and try to wait at least until dinnertime if you can." She would plead with Ms. Parson to assure that Nate would not be punished or harmed because of her.

Hannah was tired. It was late but she struggled to stay awake. Since her escape was on a Monday, she hoped Social Services would find a place before the week was out. If she had made her escape on a weekend, she would have been placed in a juvenile detention holding area at the downtown precinct—if she resisted going home. But she was willing to risk that fate rather than go back to the Wilson home. She had learned from her previous attempts how runaways were handled. Her growing desperation had given her more cunning in her escape planning.

———

WHEN NEXT TO RUN WAS EVER IN her thoughts. Last Thursday, she sensed an opportunity had come. At Mass on Thursday morning, when Father had instructed the students to pray for a special intention, Hannah had prayed to the Blessed Mother that Sister Regina would not give the seventh and eighth graders any weekend home-work, including their assigned lines of a long poem, "Invic-tus." Hannah and Nate hadn't quite mastered their three stanzas, but Sister would be pleased that they had made a good effort. Hannah needed to leave several of her heavy textbooks at school and not have to lie. She needed the space to fold an extra white uniform shirt, clean undies and socks, and her extra navy sweater in her school bag. She knew by midweek she'd try to leave. But Monday morning changed that plan; she could not wait another day.

As she was about to leave her bedroom, she heard foot-steps pass her door. The bathroom door then closed. It now seemed safe to whisk by to the stairway and down to breakfast. But within seconds, Perry, her foster brother, stepped out of the bathroom into the narrow hallway. She paused for a second but then moved closer to the banister to walk by him as quickly as she could, but Perry stood right in her path.

"Excuse me." She tried not to show her alarm. Occasionally he'd let her pass unruffled, nearly unnoticed, but not today.

"What's the hurry, little sister?" This was all too often the gauntlet of encounter. As he moved closer, she tried to move to the opposite wall. His face glistened with sweat; his thin cotton robe was half-open. Her throat began to tighten as she tried not to inhale his manly odor permeating from the open bathroom. The thought of his muscular pressure against her crisp clean school uniform would ruin the day before it had started. She felt repulsed. Soiled by just his eyes.

"Nathan, Hannah, you better hurry." Mother Wilson's irritated voice rose from the bottom of the staircase. The bedroom door just beyond the bathroom opened, and Nathan rushed out. He knocked into Perry, throwing them both off-balance for a second.

"Watch where you're going, you punk." Perry slightly shoved Nate with one arm then turned and smirked at Hannah as he barely tugged the ties of his robe near his waist.

Hannah's dampening eyes looked away. Nathan held his ground to let his sister pass, but Hannah stepped backwards into her room and firmly shut the door. Opening the top drawer of her small bureau, she quietly took out the plastic grocery bag with her provisions and placed them carefully in her book bag, which already held her loose-leaf binder. Two magazines she had borrowed from Mother Wilson's dining room were the last items she placed in the bag. The bag then had its usual shape. This was indeed the day.

———

HANNAH SAT WAITING to hear what would happen to her. Beyond the door, the two voices continued: the unwitting discredited mother and the unexpected, substitute guardian, though Hannah couldn't clearly make out the words. One voice rose and quaked, started and stopped. The other flowed evenly, stopping only when the staccato tones interrupted. Shortly only the even voice continued. There seemed to be no final refrain.

The office door opened. Ms. Parson entered the room alone. Hannah held her breath, waiting for Ms. Parson to speak.

Her social worker promised her that she wouldn't have to return to her foster home. Her words were direct, calm and kind enough. She could believe her. For the week, Hannah could be placed in a temporary parent's home. There were a few emergency settings, very few, where children could be placed overnight or sometimes for a few days. Hannah listened in silence, grateful for the words she heard. But she couldn't squelch the simultaneous roar of her hungry stomach. She cast her eyes down; Ms. Parson laughed for just a second and picked up the phone to call her contact where she hoped to take Hannah for the night. After a very short greeting, she asked if there was a space for a teenage client. How long before they might arrive, she must have been asked.

"Maybe about a little over an hour? We have one stop to make. Great, see you then."

She hung up the phone and grabbed her purse, then picked up the open folder on her desk and put it in a leather satchel. "Ever been to the Baltimore Streetcar Grill and Deli? It's my go-to place for late nights."

Hannah picked up her school bag. She felt safe for the moment and hungry. She was almost too tired to take in Ms. Parson's friendly small talk. She began to think about the food she was about to receive. She hoped to find out soon what would happen to her brother, but for now, she was thankful for this moment of sanctuary—however long it might last.

The Master Fixer and His Apprentice

THERESA BRYANT

In families, people say that traits can skip a generation. If a mother is a great seamstress, her daughter might not be able to thread a needle. If a father is athletic or handy, his son might not necessarily inherit that same aptitude or interest.

That was the case with my husband, Max, and his father, Kenny. When Max remembers his father, he often thinks of him busy at repairing his car or restoring something around the house. Whenever we visited Max's parents, Kenny was often out in the garage, searching for another tool or holding a rusted part of a machine. With a smudge of grease on his cheek, he'd be on his way to the hardware store or to a friend's farmyard to see if he could find a bolt to replace some burned-out element in an appliance.

Fixing things and fishing were Kenny Bryant's two favorite pastimes. Kenny often chose his family's dwellings by their potential for the future projects they could provide. He'd buy a house, spend two years changing broken shutters, redoing the wooden floors, replacing poorly plastered walls. Just when the house was sound, free of any flaws, Kenny would find another fixer-upper and move his wife, daughter, and son to the site of his new projects. In the small town of Lebanon, Indiana, population just about 10,000, Max attended three elementary schools and had lived in at least seven houses by the time he left for college. To trace a memory or recall a past experience, Kenny, Max, Beverly, and Elsie would first have to determine in which house they were living at the time. Was it Tripps Avenue, Otter Drive, or Maybe Sunny Brook? Barone Street was the only one Max doesn't remember.

But he recalls his father's fixing prowess and deft skill with a fishing rod with clear though mixed feelings. He has memories of his father bringing him along on his journeys to find supplies for a task. Occasionally his father would let him handle a tool until he was ready to use it. He held his son's hand as he hammered a nail to give him a sense of the swing of a hammer and the power of driving a nail into wood. He'd then pull out the nail if it wasn't straight or finish the hammering until it was level with the surface. His work was always precise, finely finished, and accurate. He took care and often drafted his work on paper. A man with just an eighth-grade education, he was a methodical craftsmen. He seemed to think with his hands. If he could touch it, he could solve the problem.

Though he never pushed, the master fixer wished he could awaken in his little apprentice the same joy he found in restoring life to an old thing, to give it a second use. He was a patient and kind man, but perhaps his student was too slow to respond.

Perhaps if the two of them worked on something new, something for Max, that might spark his son's interest. But Kenny was a fixer and a doer, not a teacher—that is what Max remembers. There was one project that he still vividly remembers. His father bought him a model airplane. The kit was rather elaborate for an eight-year-old boy. It included a small engine that demanded some additional and careful assembly. The chassis of the plane came with parts with precut grooves that had to be matched together. Max's job was to spread the parts on the worktable and to match the similar pieces. He did that task well enough. His next task was to hand the pieces to his dad as his father read the directions and looked at the diagram. First Max enjoyed the rhythm of the two-man assembly line. His father whistled a bit, talked to his son as he asked for the required pieces. Then after a while, his dad started to work faster. He began to look down for the next part himself and add it to the plane. Soon Kenny no longer asked for his son's help. The plane was slowly coming together, but the boy had no ownership in its creation. It was no longer their project. His father had made the plane. It was a plane for his son, but they hadn't built it together. Kenny completed the plane in his free time in just a few evenings, but Max no longer watched. When the plane was finished, his father proudly presented the gift to his son. Brightly painted, complete with a figurine in the cockpit.

In horror, the eight-year-old boy shrieked at the site of the helmeted pilot. It was one from a set of soldiers that belonged to Max—there were probably nearly a dozen just like it. But his father had taken the small soldier and glued it into place without asking or consulting him. He clearly wanted to make the plane special by adding one of Max's own soldiers. Both father and son misunderstood the actions of the other. To this day, Max remembers his own reaction to his father's earnest trials to pass along skills that he had learned, skills from Kenny's father and brothers. Kenny likely remembered Max's reaction for years as well.

And Kenny went on with his lessons, setting a path for

his son. He often opened a door to a task, an idea, an adventure for Max—without telling him what he was to find. And Max sometimes found the door and opened it, but often walked through without noticing, without grasping the intended lesson. Kenny built the plane, to fly the plane—with Max. The master builder, the restorer, could fix, mend, provide for his son, but he didn't know how to share the skills he treasured. Somehow his apprentice seemed to lack interest or didn't understand the lessons. Or was he afraid to fail?

Later in life, his dad continued to open doors but differently. The doors he opened for his son were the freedom to find his own interest and adventures. Some of those adventures were risky, even life-threatening, and Kenny often later remarked, "Lesson learned." Though Max appreciated the freedom to find his own adventures, would that Kenny and he had shared a few more together.

JOSIE CAROTHERS

Birth of a Radical
Let Me Introduce Jo, My Mother

Josie Carothers has always lived in a world of words. Life is so fascinating, what better way to experience it all again than to describe it? Leaving other pastimes behind— activism, socially responsible businesses, raising kids—she is now what she calls a "post-professional," living with her mate and writing, farming, and doing community service in Vermont, all with great pleasure.

Birth of a Radical (With a Subtext on Hair)

JOSIE CAROTHERS

In 1961, when I was eleven, we moved from our New England rural paradise to New Jersey, a place that I thought would be a lot more fun than it was. As a country girl, I found the suburbs confusing. Encountering for the first time the sign in the middle of town that said "Don't Walk," I thought I was following directions: I *ran*. Brakes screeched, people yelled.

But during this time of living in New Jersey, some momentous element in American culture—and I— morphed. And there was no going back.

A small kid with a little pixie haircut, I was intent on finding secret panels in our new, spooky Victorian house. Meanwhile, the big kids in my family were diving deeply into teenagerhood and the local culture. Beehive hairdos were big, but my sister Sallie would not stoop to sculpt one on her blonde head—that was for the working-class girls in town. She mastered the craft of The Flip for her hair, as was proper. She'd wash her proud blonde hair and set it in huge rollers and sleep on them. She'd ease the hair out of them and spray the turned-up ends. It was really stiff, but the look—she had it. She would give me incomprehensible advice. "Never trust the girls," she told me once. "They'll be nice to your face but rip you to shreds in the girls' room." Weren't the girls just going to the bathroom in there? Why would they "rip you to shreds"? Sallie told me that for Christmas she was going to give me something that would ensure I never got pimples. I was so disappointed. Pimples were another planet to me: I'd never be that old. Sallie had become gorgeous, successfully mastering the arts of appearance. She had scads of dates.

Johnny had become a junior-high punk with a slight squint to his eye for coolness. No more romps through the swamps, trying to trap beavers. Each morning he would comb back the sides of his hair when it was wet and encourage the front to fall down into a curl. He dried that curl plastered over his forehead by standing over the toaster, home hairdryers being a thing of the future. He tuned in to the Beach Boys and Jan and Dean and must have fancied himself a Californian at that point. Madras plaid was big, and he wore his madras shirts with carefully color-coordinated pastel pants. He was one of the coolest guys in school, never mind the grades.

Swiftie got in with the hoods at the high school. These *were* the girls with beehives, emulating the Ronnettes: *Be my, be my baby, my one and only baby, be my, be my baby—be my baby now-a-ow.* "They're so fine!" Swiftie would yell. He was always loud. The boys in his crowd were the ones too old to still be in school. They were fond of beer and breaking-and-entering. And the drive-in. They hung out at the Sip N Sup, a place you had to drive to, so I never saw it. They'd say, "We're going up the Sup," and car wheels would spin out of the driveway.

———

I STOPPED WATCHING TV. The situation comedies just weren't hitting the spot anymore. Without thinking about any of it, I took to my room and drew. And read. Ray Bradbury's science fiction stories and *A Wrinkle in Time*. The Narnia books, again.

A couple of years passed, and still what the older kids were doing had little appeal for me. Having few friends, in seventh grade I discovered Natalie Gass, the ugliest girl in the junior high. You can just imagine what the kids did with her last name. She had a low, low forehead and frizzy hair. Sallie disapproved of my new friend because she would never be popular—this would not be a success track for me. But oh, Nat was so witty! She made me laugh in new and intricate ways, and we'd howl away the nights in her ranch house's linoleum-floored basement. And she wrote poetry. Beautiful, elegant stuff. When we were fourteen, we began to explore what it meant to be profound. Our minds were boundless, that's what it felt like. She was worth the scorn of the popular kids.

The bookmobile came to school, and I bought a paperback called *Orlando* by Virginia Woolf. I didn't know this author, though there had been a play with her name in it recently. *Orlando* was about someone who lived for four hundred years. First she was a man and later, a woman. What a wild plot! Books rounded out the little world Nat and I occupied. We read teenage romances and also consumed English classics such as Yeats and Dylan Thomas, and then got our hands on *Lady Chatterley's Lover* by D.H. Lawrence for titillation. Oo-la-la!

———

NAT GASS'S father was a socialist. One night he sat us down and told us what that is. He explained the concept of social justice and how an economy could respectfully supply the needs of everybody, even the poor, if it wanted to. He gave us the pot-boiler novels of Howard Fast to reinforce his points. Nat and I *responded*. We talked deeply, beginning to accept less and less without thinking: politics, theater, humor, clothing, music. By ninth grade, all were accepted only after scrutiny. I abjured my sister's Flip, though I was old enough now to care, and the pixie was replaced by a short-and-styled. I took up the wearing of corduroy. We were blindly seeking out the unclichéd. The kids at school found us strange and did not like us, and we did not like them. But we felt meager and unappreciated under their scorn.

Then the Beatles burst upon the scene, and we were saved. It felt like they sang to *us*. Perhaps because they were foreign, perhaps because of their beautiful soft long hair, but of course because of their cheerful, new, and *expert* music, they got under our skins so deeply that we had to let it out. When Mr. Gass took us to a Beatles concert in Atlantic City, we screamed through the whole thing.

A new era was beginning. It was 1964. In another country fascinating, thoughtful people were following the example of the gentle jolly Beatles and beginning to wear their hair long. The girls from a place called Carnaby Street in London looked poetically beautiful with big eyes and long straight hair. We pored over pictures of them in *Life* magazine. England looked like a better place than the United States we knew. More seriously, though, there was a war going on in a country nobody had heard of, Vietnam. Lyndon Johnson was increasing the troop counts. It seemed to Nat and me that the war didn't make sense. Why was our country intent on establishing democracy in a little place on the other side of the world? Why couldn't they be allowed to run their own country? What's a democracy if it's forced on people? I argued about it with my mother, with my family. I made my view known in my modern European history class, and the teacher, an ex-marine, grimly made me alone debate the whole class, which was scary, but I was game. I felt some passion about this.

————

THE CRUCIAL EVENT came when I was fourteen, in 1965. Sallie had abruptly gotten married at age eighteen (I naively wrote in my journal, "Sallie decided to get married to John." I didn't suspect and they didn't tell the reason why—it was considered too shocking for me to know.) Her new husband, John Hatab, and she were living in her room at our house while Sallie's belly grew and they looked for an apartment. He was a smart and ambitious young man of twenty-two, working at a prestigious accounting firm in Newark.

One night the six of us—my parents, brother Johnny (Swiftie had been drafted into the army but safely stationed in Germany), Sallie, and John were all sitting around the big pine kitchen table eating supper. I remember the meal: mushrooms and meatballs in a wine-and-cream sauce. After a little silence punctuated by the clink of forks on plates, John began to tell about a bizarre happening from his day. During lunch, a crowd of people had gathered in the street outside his building. They carried signs and chanted, "U.S. out of Vietnam! U.S. out of Vietnam!" Huh! Why would anyone do this? Why question the government? Everyone knows that if we don't stop the Communists in Vietnam, all of Southeast Asia will fall to Communism like poking a row of dominoes standing on edge. Bunch of unpatriotic dimwits out there. He and his cohort had left their desks for the street and stood, in their suits, on the other side of the police barricade and taunted the small crowd. "America—love it or leave it!" That sort of thing. "They must have been Commies!" finished John with relish, picking up his fork. A murmur of interest moved around the table.

But I had been one of the ones in the crowd. A few days before, Mr. Gass had come to see us in Nat's basement hangout and asked if we wanted to attend. We were enthusiastic—other people thought as we did! Missing school was a bonus.

No one else was young in the little group that stood in the street that day. They were old socialists who worked in the leather factory where Mr. Gass worked. Nat and I walked back and forth with the group along the police barricade, reciting our polite chant: "U.S. out of Vietnam!" The event felt stodgy. When the young businessmen appeared and started jeering at us, we were astounded. Here we were, hoping to prevent innocent Vietnamese people from being killed by our countrymen for economic greed, and there they were, moneymen—*capitalists*— showing their blindness to others' plight, a mindless conventionality, as we saw it. I felt a vague antipathy solidi-fying to what I saw as the single-minded pursuit of money as I looked at the youths in suits. Their faces were distorted by contempt.

And there one of them was! At my dinner table! I felt shaken. I had not seen him in that group. John, still in his suit, was completing his story. I heard the others, in varying shades of agreement. Then, gathering my courage as the youngest one in the room, I spoke up—still in my school clothes of green corduroy shirt and skirt, short hair bouncing in my enthusiasm.

"John," I addressed him, "I was there. I was one of those people you were jeering at." Everyone at table was rather shocked. My mother didn't skip a beat about my not being at school. "I didn't know you *cared* so much," she commented, perhaps a little cynically. "But I do," I said. "We don't have a right to be telling people on the other side of the world what to do." Youngest though I was, I was given a fair hearing. But they shook their heads. Sallie's face showed puzzled dismay. Johnny gave me a querying look. Nobody changed their mind. They all continued to agree with John, who gazed at me with condescending pity.

Later, almost every dynamic at that table would change. But that night, deep inside myself, something fell into place that never changed.

And I started to grow my short hair long.

Let Me Introduce Jo, My Mother

JOSIE CAROTHERS

I want you to know who Jo is, while she is still alive: We're going to have fun doing this. I'm going to sneak us into her third-floor apartment to explore—snoop around!—even while she's sitting, as usual, at her dining room table, reading with her gray cat on her lap. She's pretty deaf, and if we're quiet, she won't hear us come in. But before we climb the stairs, I have a few photographs of her to show you, so you can get a hint of her life. I love my mother—you know that—and I find her to be of great interest.

Look: Here's a big close-up, artistically black-and-white. Just her face shows, and her trust in the picture-taker shows in the openness she's feeling. That was back in her seventies, and look at that broad grin, a famous grin—her wide mouth, white square teeth, and joie de vivre. I love this one.

Here's another, from the 1930s, in a large leather photo album. She's the overweight nine-year-old, a middle child standing with her three sisters. See how all of them are dressed the same, in scratchy tweed pleated skirts, wool cloches, sturdy wool-socked legs like pillars rising from stout Oxford shoes? She's the fat-cheeked one staring glumly at the camera. She grew up in wealth, intact family and all that, but missed the nurturance she had longed for. That's a complicated story.

Look at her as the slender bride—she lost the weight when she went to college, getting a break from her family. It's 1944; she is twenty-one years old. She casts her eyes down in this one, submissively posed. She's beautiful, transcendent, a thousand miles from lumpy wool. A veil of soft lace flows all the way down to the floor, a supple white silk dress drapes her seated form with the lines of a white madonna. The picture does not reveal her wit, her intellect or her warmth, but shows her young and lovely and, for the moment, willing to be fabricated into an idealization of young womanhood. She was the first one married of her four sisters, considered an accomplishment in those days even if marrying too young.

And here's a snapshot, its colors faded, of a row of chipper women in the casual long dresses of the 1960s, splashed with bright patterns: Norma, Toya, Wanda, and Jo, partying, drink glasses in hands. Middle-aged friends, having a better time with each other than with their husbands. She's the tallest one with the biggest grin.

You're right, it's true, we are not seeing the typical family portraits: kids, husband, grandchildren. That's never what fed her. Her spirit of adventure ranged her interests far and wide. Domesticity was a millstone around her neck. Yet she is capable of great kindness and understanding for her family.

Here's one of her taken just last year. This is how we see her most often these days: seated alone at her dining room table, reading, surrounded by a lifetime's artful gathering of the arcane, the beautiful and strange, a dragon's lair of a collection made by the bountiful imagination she lived to pursue. We see the woman that the objects describe. She is eighty-nine now, shrunk five inches from her broad-shouldered statuesque self, her former raven hair white and thin with pink scalp showing through. She does not often bother changing out of her nightclothes. Don't let the physical frailty fool you. Her brown eyes are shrewd. There's a full person inside.

Now we've just slipped in the door by the dining room —see, she has not heard us, she's deep into her book. She's lived contentedly alone here over thirty years, ever since she ended her archaeology period in Mexico. We're on the third floor of an 1810 Federalist red-brick, white-pillared old townhouse where she occupies the top floor in old Salem, Massachusetts. Bits of the buccaneering seafaring past are still in place in this old Yankee seaport, and that's why she lives here, for the color of the place (as well as the good memories of her old friends who lived nearby). Coming into the building, we saw that this frail remnant of a woman makes her way up two long flights of stairs to get home, often dragging bags of books. Her expeditions mainly take her to the bookshop and out to lunch at her favorite restaurant, called In A Pig's Eye, where she is known by name. I have hired someone to drive her where she wants to go these days.

We stand in the hall, peeking into her dining room. There she is, at the table heaped high with books. Books spill off the chairs, too, books on history, art, politics, a few novels. She lives to feed her mind, and she can come out with famously erudite and creative conversation if she wants to. She was a renowned conversationalist for seventy years at least, her words spiced with humor as well as insight. I see your eyes traveling to the wall of antique Mexican paintings-on-tin. They portray answered prayers, folk paintings full of disastrous events and just-in-time salvation. Does she see her life like that? She keeps so much inside, and so many disasters did happen…it's hard to know. There on the shelf is the Nanking plate brought back from the historic first American voyage to China in the eighteenth century that carried her ancestor there and back. And a huge ostrich egg engraved with the images of Emperor Maximilian and Empress Carlotta of Mexico. And a piece of eight from a pirate ship, and a row of exotic shells on a mantlepiece under an oil painting of some ancestor. Each object has a story, is weighted with meaning.

We're going to creep all the way to the back, to her bedroom, and work our way back out here. Here we are. Let's be really snoopy and look in her closet. Isn't it a strange nook! It's got a convex wall, it's wedge-shaped, it's hard to see the contents. Few modern people would put up with it, but she doesn't mind. She's not practical that way. The floor is strewn with a dusty host of flats, size 11. Huge. I happen to know that a snippy female friend of her family said eighty years ago, "Those Newton girls. Not a dainty hand or foot among them!" These things used to matter deeply. Jo had the largest feet. She couldn't shop in shoe stores with her sisters. She had to send away through the mail for her shoes: a mortification.

What clues from her dresser? It's proudly eighteenth century (a century we, her children, were brought up to love); golden wood, beautiful. Its top is saturated with dusty jewelry, almost all of it real. Ropes of pearls, boxes spilling gold, brooches of all eras punched into dusty pincushions. Masses of beaded necklaces draping hooks on the wall, cheek-by-jowl with strange Mexican wooden masks that shamans used long ago and that frightened her grandchildren. Who adore her, by the way, despite her lack of maternalism. "Pirate Granny," they call her. They understand her.

I can tell you she is a clotheshorse, even now, when she bothers. Her wardrobe includes pieces she's bought in places like Uzbekistan and Chiapas. Many of her clothes, though, are simple, to show off her jewelry. The clothes look like nothing until she puts them on. Her sense of personal style is stunning. Maybe she did have a say in how she looked in that wedding photograph, but I'd bet that confidence came later.

Her bedroom is a mess. Clothes, tissues strew about on her unmade bed. It's a sleigh bed that's been in the family for over a century, it's still got its ancient *horsehair* mattress on it, thin and hard, can you imagine? It's what she prefers. Comfort as others know it holds little attraction for her. There's a white counterpane with cat pee on it. This bedroom is like backstage at the theater with the other rooms the stage. Take a quick glance around—the photograph of her great-grandmother holding her infant grandmother is really old—but no close scrutiny, please. The errors of an old body leave embarrassing traces. But her signature perfume pervades: a not-too-sweet elixir, it clings to her scarves, books, pillowcases, letting us know to whom they belong, invading our senses with a sophisticated feminine statement. She's never liked excessive sweetness in any of its forms.

Shall we investigate the kitchen? It feels like a long walk to get there, this place is big, and when we do, I see you shiver a little. No wonder. A truly alarming array of sharp-edged antique metal hand choppers lines the walls, like little guillotines waiting to fall. The shapes are eclectic; I can see why she likes them. Yet the feng shui just doesn't please, does it? And, yes, there is that disquieting lineup of long knives dangling from a Mexican knife-holder on the wall. Nobody likes this room but she. As a person she has been notably nonviolent, even in the turbulence of our family as I was growing up. Maybe this is the room of her shadow self, a buccaneer.

Her living room is heavenly, though. Gorgeous. Look at the rich royal blue walls—a statement color she always painted her living rooms—and pure white molding. A black marble fireplace dramatizes one wall, and a bookcase takes up an entire other wall. Heaps of tiny antiquities in silver bowls sit on three-hundred-year-old tavern tables. I am not the only one who, even though seeing many of these objects all my life, still paws through the bowls in fascination whenever I visit. Ancient Roman glass, ivory dice, early American marbles, medieval coins, Czech glass beads, and weird bits of old Mexicana and who-knows-what rub together in the bowls and they compel us all. My children play dice games to win their choice of objects from the bowls when they visit, then they put them back. They are adults now, but they still do it. We love these objects not just for what they are but for the spirit which drove the collecting of them: endless curiosity, time-travel, inventiveness. With these things she showed a world to us all, a world that in no small way shaped the lives of her children and grandchildren, despite the lack of maternal presence. It was her world—that, and her knowledge that could knit it all together into uncommon patterns with the ring of truth.

Time to slip out now. We'll creep past the door to the dining room—see, she never looked up from her reading...

I am so glad you let me show you Jo's uncommon world. On the doorstep now, I want to tell you: She is worth knowing. She represents to our family the standard of an *educated* mind, separate from shallow trends: a cultured human being. Her frustration with the lot of marriage and children came from a spirit that wanted to play on a wider stage. Her discernment, her sense of humor that could erupt into her characteristic loud laugh, her gravitas, her bearing are all worth preserving. When I was growing up, she used to speak poetry to me, from Gerard Manley Hopkins to A.A. Milne to Kipling and Lawrence, in her deep, mannish voice. She dislikes that voice as she dislikes most things about her physical self, which would surprise anyone who has known the public Jo, but that's the survival of the fat, glum child in the picture, whose mother didn't like her. Her sense of beauty in poetry, in all things, was a saving grace for her. That is why her things describe her.

Immured up there with her books, you might wonder at her character. Though she was curious about these things, she came from a time when the self-awareness of psychology hadn't taken hold yet, let alone feminism. Other things reigned in her formative years: the grand ideas, duty, heroism, classical music, discernment, the enduring social institutions. Pens, fine paper, girdles and garters and good grammar. Aspiration to achieve at standards inspirational as well as oppressive. In some ways, knowing Jo is time-travel to a *nobler* epoch. In other ways, she simply shows us the universals. Love, endurance, betrayal, laughter. And her irrepressible determination to be herself, whatever the cost.

Old age finds her no longer able to reliably deploy the wit that delighted her large collection of almost all-gone-now friends. Like the knight who always won, Jo's spear of personality lifted her pride and she excelled at the joust. But now the lance is too heavy to lift and just occasionally she'll hoist it and parry, to the aching delight of her visitors. She is the glory of our family, and, as used to be said about great people, we will not see her like again.

PAM CORCORAN

Ireland
My Animals
My Life With Cancer
New York City
Wonder

I was born November 22, 1950, in Bridgeport, Connecticut, one of three girls, the youngest. I started writing when
I kept my diary and journals as a young girl growing to an
adult, which provided my interest in writing. I've always
wanted to be a writer. My dream is to write my whole life
story. I would like my family to have this memory of me. I
grew up in Stratford, Connecticut. I spent most of my life
in Connecticut. From Stratford I went to live in Bridgeport, New Haven, then Meriden. I came to live in Vermont
when I found out I had breast cancer. My sister wanted me
to be near her for my treatments. To this day, I am cancer-
free.

Ireland

PAM CORCORAN

I had a dream I went to Ireland. It was so beautiful. I had a tour guide who showed me, all in all, the Ireland I had always wanted to go to.

The tour guide showed me all the different churches, all of the historical sights, even store windows where you could buy gifts to take back home, little trinkets, even the waterfalls, so very beautiful.

I remember going into the churches and feeling that peace come over me knowing in prayer.

I remember the tour guide, the Irish pub where you could get Irish whiskey, Irish soda bread, the restaurants, good Irish meals. You could get corn beef and cabbage, Irish soda bread—my mother used to make it when she was alive.

I remember getting a DVD of Irish music I could listen to over and over again. How I love Irish music. I could get little gifts to take home to my friends.

All in all I loved the sunrise, the beautiful blue sky, the sun, just having the clouds.

I couldn't believe I was in Ireland, a place I always wanted to go and visit, a place I would never forget. It had such beauty. A place I want to visit over and over again. I would never have grown tired of it. All in all I never grow tired of Ireland.

My Animals

PAM CORCORAN

I grew up with lots of cats. My favorite cat was Georgine. She was black and white. She loved to cuddle up to me. It hurt me so much when I had to put her to sleep. We had so many of them, so we had to put them to sleep. Then I had Thomasina, named her after the movie *The Three Lives of Thomasina*. She was also so cuddly and lovable. I had to get rid of her because I was in an abusive situation. It hurt me terribly to get rid of her. My sister's mother-in-law took her. When she died Thomasina wouldn't eat, so my sister had to put her to sleep. She was also so very cuddly and lovable. I loved her to death.

Then I had Rascal, the last cat I had. I had him in Connecticut. I took him to Vermont with me. He was also cuddly and lovable. It upset me terribly when he was sick and I had to put him to sleep.

I also grew up with a dog, a beagle named Ripley. He didn't like to be disturbed when he was sleeping. Both myself and my sister bent down to kiss him, and he nipped my mouth and my sister's lips and sent us to the hospital. We were hurting for a while. We overcame our hurt. Ripley was a mean dog in many ways, also a lovable dog in many ways.

All in all I will always remember all the cats and dogs I grew up with. They will always hold a special place in my heart.

My Life With Cancer

PAM CORCORAN

My unshakable memory I had was when I was first diagnosed with breast cancer. It blew my socks off. I was very much in shock and all I could think was I am going to die. But they got it in time. I had to go through surgery to remove my left breast. There were two tumors in it. Thank goodness they got it all. I was shaken at the thought of losing my breast. It had to be done. The chemo and radiation took a toll on me. They were very hard to go through, especially the chemo. I had no taste for anything. The radiation wasn't bad. It just made marks on my body where my breast was. It was an unforgettable experience waiting to hear if they really got it all, an experience I put behind me. I had to have a special breast implant, a special bra for the rest of my life, like my mother, who died of lung cancer. It was an experience I will never forget. To this day, I am cancer-free.

New York City

PAM CORCORAN

I remember very well my trips to NYC. The Empire State Building—what a big building! My ride on the train from Meriden, Connecticut—a long ride, at least five hours. Getting off the train, walking from the train station all the way to Manhattan, a long walk. All of the stores along the way.

The Statue of Liberty: What a beautiful thing! Walking up the stairs to the top of the Statue of Liberty. It is so very beautiful.

I also went to Central Park. What a beautiful park to walk through, so quiet and peaceful. Students studying there.

Rockefeller Center, another nice place to visit. Times Square, another nice place to visit.

I remember Chinatown. How I love Chinese food. The different shops with Chinese things in them. I didn't buy anything. Lovely to look at, especially the Chinese New Year, a grand celebration, all the noise in the streets. Sitting in the Chinese restaurant and how the dust flew into the restaurant while you were eating. There was nothing you could do about it. Part of the Chinese custom.

Several lovely churches to go to mass and pray.

All in all, it was quite an experience in New York City.

Wonder

PAM CORCORAN

I recently read the book *Wonder*, a story about a young boy who had a disfigured face. He felt no one would like him or accept him. He grew up, went through school, and graduated. He was so very wrong. Everyone accepted him for the way he was. He made many friends. His disfigured face would live on. Nothing he could do about it but accept himself for who he was. It makes me think of myself.

I felt when growing up I wouldn't be accepted because I was slower than my sisters in school. I graduated, but not on grade level. I was a very slow learner. I couldn't keep up with my sisters. They were smarter than I was. It was hard on my father. He could never accept me for who I was. I had a hard childhood growing up with my sisters. It wasn't easy. My father favored my sisters more because they were smarter than I was. He could never accept me for who I was.

I hope to see the movie *Wonder* soon when it comes to Randolph. I really enjoyed the book. The boy hid his face so people wouldn't have to look at him and make them sick inside. All in all, he was very smart. He knew he was accepted. All in all, a very moving book indeed. I will never forget it. By reading the book you can tell he was hurting inside. How people came to accept him for who he was. A very good book to read.

LYDIA ENGLISH
Spring
Transformations

Lydia had an important writing mission when she joined the group in 2010. Many important family stories had been passed from one generation to another. She had to get these stories, particularly those of the women, into written form. *A Women's Legacy of Spirit, Love, and Fancy: From the Hold of a Slave Ship to the Ivy League* was published in 2011.

Lydia was born in Chicago. She worked at Independence Bank of Chicago after graduating from high school. In 1969, she moved to Saint Thomas in the U.S. Virgin Islands to continue her banking career and to get away from the midwest winters. She left Saint Thomas eight years later to attend Brown University, where she earned a degree in social cultural anthropology and followed that up at Yale University with a PhD in the same discipline. She worked as a faculty member at Brown and as a Dean of the sophomore class before accepting a position at the Andrew W. Mellon Foundation, where she completed her career as a philanthropist.

Spring

LYDIA ENGLISH

Begin again . . .
Spring is a slate wiped clean, a new day . . . we begin again.

In my imagination of spring, the air is clear, the sky is blue, and lilacs are the air's perfume. It is a bit like New Year's Eve in that life begins anew.

I have always been happy that my birthday is in May. It is a time each year for me to review the year past and plan for the next. This review includes meditation on my values with the possibility of revising those behaviors that are either negative or just not helpful.

Sometimes I find myself going all the way back to my childhood to examine the genesis of certain behaviors. Sometimes this is a positive experience and I rejoice in my growth and good decisions. "Spring forward" is a good motto. Move into awareness, look for answers, think of the questions. I regain a love for life and all of the possibilities.

It took me many years to realize that I am in charge of me. I have made plenty of mistakes or blunders, but some have turned out to be gifts to my soul. Many years ago, I had a terrible auto accident. I nearly died, but instead after months of recuperation, I came fully alive. I learned who I really am, what I believe in, and what I dream for myself. This time of reflection was a wakeup call for me. It made me appreciate life each and every day.

Spring reminds me of this time of reflection and rejuvenation. I relish my spirit, the people in my life, and the reappearance of green grass and flowers. I love these writing groups because I never know what I am going to write about. Thank you for the inspiration.

Transformations

LYDIA ENGLISH

In 1999, I moved to New York City from Providence, Rhode Island. After living in a rental apartment for two years, I was ready to think about buying my own property in Manhattan, which would lessen my commute to work. I did so at Seward Park on the Lower East Side. Here is how that happened:

Coincidently, Ms. Joan Fox from Corcoran Realty called me at work to tell me about an apartment for sale. Athough we had spoken once before, we had not spoken for some time, so I was surprised. She had just listed an apartment, and thought I might be interested. I agreed to go with Ms. Fox to see the apartment she described.

That very afternoon, we went together to see the apartment. It was dark and dingy; the windows were cloudy from constant sun exposure. You could barely see out of them. The bathroom was nasty; the tub was rusty, and the toilet was stained beyond repair. There was a threadbare rug covering the living room and bedroom floors. The apartment was a mess, but it had a small balcony overlooking the East River and the FDR Drive. The living room and bedroom windows also faced this lovely view.

My assistant, Carma, accompanied me on this visit. Her face told me I should forget about this place. The more I looked around, though, the more potential I could see. I asked about the price, which seemed too high, but learned that the seller was the daughter of a woman who lived in the apartment until her death. The seller lived in Florida, so I suspected she would be willing to negotiate. She was, and the deal was closed.

MY NEW APARTMENT was located at 266 East Broadway in something called the Seward Park Cooperative. It was a few blocks from Chinatown in a largely Jewish residential neighborhood. Most of the residents of the building were from the Hasidic Jewish sect. As a result, they were among the orthodoxy. The building, although now open to people of other faiths, always maintained respect for its orthodox residents. For example, the elevators were programmed on Friday sundown through Saturday sundown to stop on every floor so that the faithful would not have to violate the strict rules of their religion and press the button for their floor.

The Cooperative Complex was built in the early sixties to house garment workers. It was composed of four buildings, each with twenty floors. My building was two blocks from the F train, which I rode to and from work every day. My new apartment was on the twelfth floor. In addition to having a gorgeous view of the East River, I looked out upon both the Manhattan and the Williamsburg bridges.

I immediately started working on my new home. I had all of the windows replaced; the beautiful parquet floors cleaned, sanded, and refinished; tiles laid in the kitchen and bathroom; and complete repainting of the interior. I chose a Santa Fe red for one of the accent walls in the living room and a faint gold for the remaining walls and the hallway. The bedroom was painted baby blue and the bathroom was a retro black and white with all new fixtures and a new vanity. I painted the kitchen a sunny yellow with beige cabinets. I put in a new sink, stove, and granite counter top. When Carma came over again three weeks later, she could not believe the transformations. The apartment was beautiful, and I loved it.

THERE WERE eight apartments on my floor. Next door to me, facing out to the river, was a middle-aged Jewish couple, Sheldon and Elaine. Leading down the hallway next to the two elevators were Tim and Jeff, two eccentric mid-thirties white men. On the other side of the corridor was a Hispanic woman and her Chinese husband with their two preteen children. The apartment next to them was empty for the entire eight years that I lived in the building. Lastly, a single Jewish woman occupied the only three-bedroom apartment on the floor. The building and the neighborhood were diverse.

The neighbors weren't particularly sociable, and we did not ever visit each other's apartments. We only saw one another in the hallway or by the elevators, but just from those brief encounters I got to know a little about them. The two men, Tim and Jeff, were cat lovers—and probably lovers. Every couple of weeks they received a bulk order of cat litter and cat food. I could never determine how many cats they had, but it was more than three. Periodically, they would have a disagreement that took them out into the hall screaming and pounding each other. Then there were Sheldon and Elaine next door who were quiet as mice during the week, but on weekends they played their doo-wop music late into the night and began their ritual screaming insults at each other. The other tenants on my floor were quiet and peaceful—although Mrs. Rodriguez, who lived next to Tim and Jeff, seemed to cook beans and rice every day, which I smelled on my way in from work. All this was my indoor neighborhood.

MY OUTDOOR NEIGHBORHOOD was lively and loud; nighttime was the loudest. Around midnight most nights there seemed to be a fire somewhere in the neighborhood, because fire engines constantly screeched through the streets, blaring their sirens. I would jump out of bed to see where they were going, but I never saw any fire or smoke, so I would go back to bed. Car alarms were another source of irritation. For some reason, which I never discovered, car alarms would go off in a rash every night. Then there were the barking dogs. The night was a cacophony of the most horrendous noises. I finally had to resort to earplugs.

The daytime was different. On my way to work every morning I passed a playground right next to the subway where elderly Chinese people were doing the most beautiful Tai Chi movements to beautiful soothing flute music playing on their portable radios. Their music and movements seemed to quiet my spirit for the start of my day. Behind the building was a lovely gated grassy playground area that had benches, chess tables, and a play area for children. Every day I would come through this park area after work and see the children playing, the old men playing chess or dominoes, and people lying on the grass quietly reading. It was a beautiful bucolic scene in the middle of the city's frenzy.

I would finish my workday sitting on my balcony with a

cool glass of wine, looking out at the glimmering water of the East River with the big and small boats gliding by. People always think that New York City is a crazy place to be, but for me some of my most peaceful moments were spent at my apartment on the Lower East Side, especially as I watched the golden globe of the sun rise every morning over the river's horizon.

JOAN FEIERABEND

Release
When I Asked

AN AUTOBIOGRAPHY IN 126 WORDS: Born in Poughkeepsie on 8/19/43 the youngest of three girls, lived youth in Red Hook, NY, 1962 entered Pratt Institute and moved to Brooklyn, NY, 1966 married Richard Dybvig, 1969 earned my BFA Pratt Institute, 1969 taught deaf blind 5 year olds, 1970 moved to Tunbridge VT, taught at Goddard and VT college in their adult degree programs, 1973 birthed Dana, 1975 birthed Evan, 1978–1980 taught kindergarten, 1980 separated, 1981 began teaching k-12 art in Chelsea, VT, 1988 divorced, 1993 MFA VT college, 2007 retired, 2002 became a grandmother to Owen, 2004 Louis, and 2006 Rose, 2016 moved from Tunbridge to East Randolph.

I live comfortably with myself, searching life's meaning through painting, drawing, sculpting, and writing.

Release

JOAN FEIERABEND

I t happened in the summer of '81. I remember the year because it was the summer my ex-husband and I had separated after sixteen years of marriage. Our lives were still quite interlocked, not only because we have two children together but also because he had an office and I a studio in the same house in town. Dick was living in the house we built together out on Russell Road, and I had moved with the children (at the time aged eight and six) to the small apartment above the office and studio.

That morning, I had just taken the children to day camp and was returning to the studio to work. Dick was already in his office on the floor below me. It was a day like any other summer day, warm, sunny, and slow to begin.

When I walked into the studio I heard a rustling noise followed by some muffled squawking. Tracking the sound, I noticed movement in a glass jar that was sitting on the windowsill. It was one of those gallon jugs with a small hole for pouring and a glass loop handle right next to the opening. As I drew closer and carefully peered into the jar I could see two large black birds scrabbling against the glass and each other filling the jar completely with their bulk. As I approached, their terror escalated. I could see their feathers pressed hard against the glass, a beak squished against the surface distorting the bird's mouth. Both birds were squawking and ramming their feet against the glass and each other, frantic with the need to escape. I felt as if I was watching an accident happening, powerless to prevent injuries. Shocked and dazed I immediately went downstairs to get Dick to help me figure out what to do about this bizarre situation.

Breaking the jar wasn't an option. Surely injury would result from that. At last we settled on laying the jar on its side, outside in the shaded grass, out of harm's way, and leaving the birds to work their way out alone.

We went back inside to see if we could puzzle out the mystery. On close inspection of the studio, the only thing out of the ordinary was a piece of izen glass lying on the floor next to the antique Round Oak stove. Sure enough, the stove had an empty window hole. Surely the birds had come down the stovepipe and, feeling trapped, by the dark barrel of the stove's center, saw the light through the izen glass and poked it clean out. Still looking for a nice little hole in which to hide their nest, the birds had found the lip of the jar and squeezed in, first one and then its mate. After that, they were stuck. Once we felt we had solved the riddle we went outside and found the jar empty. Just as we hoped, the quiet, peaceful view of the outside world allowed them to relax and find their way out to be free.

We eventually identified the birds as grackles, a stretched version of the common blackbird. I think freeing them helped Dick and me as we let each other go from the grips of a restricting marriage. Whether we needed that little metaphor from nature to guide us or not, I've always seen the liberation of those birds as our role model for how to part. Thirty-three years later, I can say we did well.

An addendum to this story happened about six months ago. Two years earlier, all my writing was lost in a computer crash. Nancy Reid suggested I use "Realease" for this booklet. Remarkably, she found a copy of it in her email archives, a full three years after I had written it. On impulse, really, I sent a copy to Dick.

"I had forgotten all about that incident," he said. "You did a nice job writing about it, but I thought there was only one bird."

When I Asked

JOAN FEIERABEND

I arrived home from grocery shopping one day to find what appeared to be a piece of unsplit firewood sitting upright on my front porch. Although it didn't make sense, I thought it might have been put there by my on-again, off-again lover, Mark, who is a woodsman. A closer look revealed it wasn't a piece of firewood at all. It appeared to be a sculpture of sorts, for it had a recessed cover made of stone, probably slate, cut into a circle that had been divided into three pieces, which fit together like a jigsaw puzzle. This three-stoned lid rested on a lip carved into the wood, allowing the stones to lie flush with the top of the wood. You could only see the stonework from above.

Perplexed and curious, I reached down and wedged my finger into a space between the wood and one of the stones, lifting it carefully. After that, all three stones lifted easily to reveal a conical recess about three inches deep at its center. There was a small piece of paper, which appeared to be litter, for it had that unmistakable look of a cast-aside candy wrapper that had been living in the elements for a while. The ugly red, yellow, and blue graphics were all crinkled and almost worn off. On the back of the wrapper, written in blue ballpoint pen, were the words "for Joan." This was one of those moments that caught in my throat a swelling from my heart, a life's work affirmed. At once I knew it was from one of my former students, Will, who had continued his studies in art after high school using materials from nature and recycling bins. I brought the sculpture inside and found a place where I would see it as I entered the house. How does a teacher thank a student for such a gift? I know I wrote something on a hand-drawn card, but I know my words were inadequate.

It is within the cavern of this cherished gift that I have placed in evidence another gift that materialized out of the soil like an offering from the gods, at my request, a private miracle.

What essential ingredients were aligned that cold October dusk? Perhaps need, desire, and a hit of desperation created the assembly of energies to manifest my subsequent gift.

The scene for my miracle took place in my mother's garden one evening in late October. Mom was nearing the end of six weeks of daily radiation treatments after her surgery for colon cancer. We had prepared ourselves well for her to heal, wearing out our Bernie Siegel tapes, doing the weekly exercises together in *The Artist's Way,* writing our morning pages, and going on our artists' dates. Mom had made it through the surgery admirably, but the process for keeping a positive attitude on this blustery October evening was wearing a little thin. Mom was increasingly drained from the radiation, and her tiredness made her a little grouchy with me for not having finished planting the "Double Works" bundle of two hundred perennials from White Flower Farms in her untilled hillside garden. Mom had ordered them the previous spring before her cancer had been diagnosed. Their late arrival for a fall planting in Vermont made her fretful. School had begun for me, and I had been hacking away at the planting, but the ground was full of the most entrenched weeds and grass. My progress was slow. With the shortening days and a bit of snow falling, I realized I'd better finish the job that evening even though I was exhausted after a full day of teaching. The pressure of taking care of my mom and her lawns and gardens as well as my own was becoming overwhelming. I was also feeling irritated at her laying her stress on me about getting the job done. As usual there was guilt. I should be doing everything diligently without irritation— with love.

I had been working about forty minutes, and even so, the limp pile of plants looked just as huge as it did when I started. At my feet was a huge clump of grass that would take at least four prying moves with the shovel before it would break free. I looked up at the darkening sky, ignoring the snowflakes that were falling on my face. "God," I wailed, "I need a sign that I am doing the right thing here." I stood there for a minute. Who was I to ask for a sign from a God whose existence for me was a word more than a belief? Wearily, I jammed the shovel into the grass. I was right; it took four pries to loosen the rooted grip. I bent down to shake out the dirt. There was something white wedged in the roots and dirt. I took off my gardening gloves and worked my cold, wet fingers into the gritty soil to get a better hold on the object. I pulled it free and wiped the dirt on my mud-soiled sweats before I looked to see what I had found. To my astonishment, I was holding a plastic angel playing a violin.

All resistance to the work melted away as I finished the job with what felt like ease. It was full dark when I met my mom's worried face. With a big smile on my face I announced, "I'm finished, and look what I found!" I showed Mom the angel. I didn't tell her the lead-up to finding it. Did she need to know how desperate I felt? I urged her to take the angel, but she said I should keep it. Perhaps she knew how much I needed it after all.

The flowers came up straight and tall the following spring, and Mom was well enough to lovingly tend them for two more years before the cancer claimed her.

Now when I feel the need, I lift the three-stone lid from my unique sculpture and take out the little white angel so I can remember what it taught me: Do my best, even when it is very difficult, and when I have the need for energy from a source greater than my own, I can ask.

PAT MENCHINI

Early Bird Bowling
That One Guest

Pat joined the writing group in 2013 just after her retirement from a twenty-four-year career at Vermont Technical College. She had one goal in mind: She wanted to write the Vermont Tech nursing program history; she would complete this rather dry writing assignment and step away. She never left. After a long career as a nurse and as a faculty member and college administrator, she found writing to be cathartic and the group to be so supportive that leaving was not an option.

Pat was born and raised in Pittsfield, Massachusetts. She graduated from Wagner College in 1969 with a baccalaureate in nursing and from Russell Sage College in 1995 with a master's degree in nursing. She lived and worked as an RN in New York City, on Long Island, in southern New York State, and in Vermont. The position from which she retired in 2012 was Dean of Academic Affairs at Vermont Tech, a job she loved, but one that she found challenging and exhausting at the same time!

.

Early Bird Bowling

PAT MENCHINI

About a year ago, a good friend asked me if I would be interested in joining her Monday-morning bowling league. They had lost a member, and she thought it might be a fun experience for me. Bowling! The last time I bowled was when I was thirteen years old. My parents entered me into a Saturday-morning league because they liked bowling and hoped we would be able to bowl as a family. I enjoyed it but later gave it up for Saturday-morning roller skating. I had not bowled in more than fifty years, and I wondered if I would be able to handle the heavy balls. That said, it sounded like a challenge, so I said yes!

Early one morning in late summer, my friend and I arrived at the Valley Bowl in Randolph, Vermont. The lanes are in an off-the-beaten-path location behind the Chandler Music Hall and under the Prince Street bridge. The building is next to the local food shelf and a restaurant that has an uneven reputation for food quality. It is a low-slung gray clapboard-sided structure with a red, white, and blue Coca Cola sponsorship sign over the entrance. In addition, a red, white and blue "Open" flag hangs from the doorframe.

In we went. My first impression was "Yikes, how seedy!" A wall of bowling lockers faces all who enter. The lockers alternate between blue and off-white; each one is about eighteen inches square. They need repainting as they are dirty looking and scratched. Shelving on top of the lockers houses bowling balls of various colors and weights for those who don't have their own equipment. Initially, I was one of those who needed to use a house ball and rent house shoes. It was hard to find a ball that was not too heavy! I searched and searched and they all felt like I would not be able to roll them down the lane. The shoes were okay. They were red and green and the owner sprayed them with what I assume was disinfectant…a bit creepy, but I had socks on, so that gave me some confidence that all would be well. I admit to wondering just how many feet had preceded mine in these rental shoes!

On the left of the reception desk is an eating space: a small café with about six white Formica tables and soda-shop chairs. A reception counter and a cash register are in the middle of the space. Behind that is a kitchen. The menu consists of simple hot and cold sandwiches, soft drinks, wine, and beer.

All ten lanes are on the right. Behind every two lanes is a seating area. No desk for scoring is included because scores are now computer generated and managed if necessary at the reception desk. In other words, if the bowler notices a scoring error, it is corrected by notifying the person managing the reception desk, and the change is made centrally. Adding scores is no longer necessary! This is a big change from the old days!

I have now been bowling for a year—every Monday at 8:30 AM. My friend moved away, but I stayed with the sport. I enjoy it. I like the exercise and the fact that I keep getting better. I now have my own equipment. I can predict the trajectory of the ball and can determine why and how I score what I do on each roll.

The early morning crowd consists of nine teams of two; three men and fifteen women. Most of the women are retired. A couple of the women are young enough to be working, but I don't think they are. The men are in their thirties and forties. At least one works an evening job at Denny's, but I don't think the others are employed. The culture at the bowling lanes is one of not asking any personal questions beyond, "Hi, how are you today?" As a result, I don't know much about any of the bowlers' personal lives.

The men are very touchy-feely. Hugs are not uncommon; sometimes they sneak up behind you. Kisses on the cheek occur occasionally. It is a very odd and uncomfortable situation. Once the bowling starts, all that touchy stuff stops and people just bowl. Each week, two teams compete. The scores are cumulative with first, second, and third places announced at the end of each 30-week session. The environment is supportive with each player rooting even for those on competing teams.

The events of one week stand out. This is what happened. My team partner was ill. The sub was a young man who was pleasant, chattier than is typical of the male bowlers, and an encouraging partner. He did not offer advice, but I noticed right away that he was an excellent bowler, so I asked for some pointers. He gladly gave them. In the first game, I noted that he bowled five strikes in a row. A perfect score is 12 strikes consecutively. He was his pleasant self as he continued to rack up strike after strike. Soon, the lanes became quiet and people from the other lanes started to watch his progress very carefully. After 10 strikes, there was a crowd gathered behind our lanes. I was nervous for him. Anyway, after 11 strikes, my partner's ball failed to return. The return of each ball is also centrally generated, so we told the person at the reception desk and he went to work on figuring out the problem. The delay felt endless. Finally, the ball came back and he took his final throw. Another strike…a perfect game! A bowler's wildest dream! The place erupted with applause, cheers and hugs for the perfect-score bowler! The receptionist called the paper and someone came down and took some action shots. It was such a thrill!

Suffice it to say that the bowling league is one in which I didn't have any preconceived notions of what it might be like, nor did I think I would stick with it very long. But we all like each other and get a kick out of each other's success. Now, I look forward to Monday mornings, to bowling camaraderie, to improving albeit minimally, and to having fun in a place and in a sport that I did not think would bring me this much pleasure!

That One Guest

PAT MENCHINI

It was a chilly October Friday-night birthday-party dinner gathering at the home of the birthday girl. She was turning fifty-nine. The party was planned by her female partner of twenty-five years and was touted to all invitees as a relaxing and festive occasion. There were three female couples and one male-female couple in attendance. We were enjoying some delicious hors d'oeuvres and a glass of wine in the living room. All were chatting companionably.

Those in attendance were all successful in their work lives, enjoying leadership positions. Four of us were registered nurses now working in administrative or nursing faculty positions. Two were ordained clergy, one was a photographer, and one was a program officer at a major New York City foundation. I mention this to set the stage for my confusion regarding our combined lack of response as one of the guests decided to commandeer the party.

As amiable and pleasant conversation continued in the living room, suddenly the only gentleman in the room stood up and said, "Here is what we are going to do! We are going to go around the room and all say what is the most beautiful city we have visited and why." I was struck by this person's need to take over the conversation. The party was not for him, nor were we in his home. No one had been sitting silently or awkwardly unengaged in conversation. That said, several of us knew each other fairly well, but none of us knew him that well. We were all smiling at him, but I imagine there were others who were as taken aback by his sudden takeover as I was.

The next thing we all knew this man was calling on individuals to participate in the favorite-city-and-why conversation. I found myself feeling irritated, but I jumped right in when he called my name. What was going on here? Why were we all participating even though there had been no need for this icebreaker activity? I still don't know. I will admit that the cities that people mentioned resulted in continued conversation as people shared their own experiences with visiting those same cities or asked questions about them, resulting in conversations that would not have come up without this exercise and yet, I couldn't shake my irritation that we were all kowtowing to this takeover.

As we were called into dinner, this guest continued to place himself in the role of leader of the group and conversation. Tell us all what was the hardest thing you ever had to do in your job. How did you meet your spouse? Was it because he was the only male and therefore saw himself as the alpha dog? The truth is that all of the females were more successful in our work lives than he, but we all acquiesced. He led the conversation throughout dinner and although he did allow the birthday girl to lead a discussion regarding what she was thankful for at this particular birthday, as soon as there was a lull, he jumped back into the leadership role.

I suppose our unified reluctance to do nothing had

everything to do with not disturbing a celebratory event with a confrontation, but in retrospect it felt distressing to me that we let this happen. This guest took control and did not relinquish it all evening and we just surrendered. What could we have done? I'm not sure. Perhaps I could have said something like, "What an interesting idea (to discuss cities of beauty and why), so why don't we all think about it and have a brief conversation about it after dinner? Meanwhile, what would the birthday girl like to talk about?" That would have shut him down gently and placed the star of the event back in control. Sadly, I did not say that nor did any of us.

It is hard to justify our behavior in the setting of this birthday event. It is hard to justify his behavior too. The feeling of powerlessness to change the events of the evening without causing a stir were prominent in my thinking as I suspect it was with others. We were just as complicit in giving him power as he was in taking it? Were we all just being good girls?

LINDA MORSE

A Moonlit Night
Skiing Through Life

Linda, a born-and-raised Vermonter, lived much of her adult life in California but is pleased to be living back in the hills of Vermont with her husband. She loves hiking, walking, and skiing the hills of home and its splendid seasonal changes. She began writing later in life and has focused on family members and how these men and women fit into her family's story. Vermont's landscape and its distinct seasons form the backdrop of her writing.

A Moonlit Night

LINDA MORSE

The deep, haunting sound of the Tibetan horn carried through the evening dusk and echoed off the snow-covered mountains of the Mount Everest region. In the Tengboche Monastery, located at an altitude of 12,600 feet in the Kumbu region of Nepal, Sherpa people, drawn by the sound of the horn, were gathering in the dark central courtyard. On this cold November evening they were slowly forming a large circle. Dozens of warmly dressed men and women faced inward with arms lined across shoulders.

Along with a small group of my fellow American trekkers, I was seated in the open upper gallery of the monastery with a view of the circle forming below in the darkened courtyard. As the drums started a slow, mesmerizing beat, the men and women began moving slowly to the right, their booted feet stamping out a regular rhythm. Their low chanting created a steady drone.

I looked out over the high walls of the monastery as the full moon rose, highlighting the icy flanks of Everest, as well as the neighboring peaks of Lotse and Nupste. This gathering of the local Sherpa people was part of the Tibetan Mani Rumdu Festival, celebrated every year for several days at the full moon in November. Gone were the colorful sand mandalas of the previous days' festivities, as well as the ritual comic dancing and mock fights of the grotesque masked dancers and the chanting with the head lama of the monastery. Instead, this moonlit night carried a meditative sense of community among the gathered Sherpas.

My trekking group had set out from the tiny Nepalese airstrip at Lukla eight days earlier. This three-day stopover was our first real break. Everything had merged to create an aura of peaceful vibrancy: our daily physical exertion; the high altitude; the striking presence of the Tibetan Buddhist stupas; spinning prayer wheels; red, yellow, and blue prayer flags fluttering in the thin air; and the warm faces of our Sherpa hosts.

As I looked down from my balcony seat, sadness about the death of my mother six months earlier, and a growing sense that my current love relationship was poised at a turning point, formed my emotional backdrop for the peaceful atmosphere in the monastery courtyard. Bathed in the cool moonlight, the rotating circle below and the guttural chanting voices created in me a deepening peacefulness tinged with melancholy. Soon enough I became immersed in the slow mesmerizing movement, the moonlit scene in the courtyard, and the sound of prayerful chanting and the shuffling boots of the Sherpas.

The next day my fellow trekkers and I would gather our gear, don hiking boots and thick down parkas, and continue our journey to the Everest basecamp, accompanied by the quiet chanting of the Sherpa porters and the gentle clanging of bells on the necks of our sturdy pack animals. But below me in this moon-drenched scene of the monastery courtyard, I was completely present to every nuance of frigid night air, the smell of cooking fires, the rhythmic chanting of the gathered Sherpas, and moonlight illuminating the snow-covered flank of Everest.

Skiing Through Life

LINDA MORSE

I n the Mad River Glen ski lift line, on the ski slopes with family and friends or even with strangers, my older brother Phil likes to engage with people. A question about the kind of skis, a kidding comment to a youngster barely big enough to get on the chairlift—he loves to learn, laugh, and connect with people. Life is more rich and fun that way.

Phil and Norma, my older sister, are both gregarious and outgoing. Surprising, given the quiet nature of our father, Leslie, and the gracious, polite manner of our mother, Florence. As a young man and throughout his life, Phil has always had a genial personality and joking ways of engaging with people. Whether he is teasing a sister younger by fourteen years; Carol, his wife of four decades; a thirteen-year-old grandson; a stranger waiting to board the double chairlift on a snowy winter day; a hardware store clerk selling him a new tool; a Creek Street neighbor stopping by for a casual chat; a physical therapist removing staples from his leg after knee surgery—all are interesting to talk with, sometimes for only a few brief seconds, or perhaps even fair game for a longer story. Phil is interested in the world around him and the people he meets. He will sing old-timey songs for elders at a senior facility, peppering his performance with chatty comments and pithy vignettes. He can be gracious and caring when called upon to support people in his life.

A particularly gnarly Vermont ski trail with broad patches of ice at Mad River Glen can throw one off balance or even result in a spectacular wipeout with gloves and poles in one direction and skis scattered in another. As with most of us, life has sometimes tossed Phil tough circumstances, even ones fraught with disappointment. Difficult decisions have generally led him to make caring choices. He has learned life lessons and ways of approaching these inevitable ups and downs. At eighty-four, he is beset with bothersome health issues but seems to keep his sense of humor, while still acknowledging that "getting old ain't for sissies."

Skiing, as a metaphor, mirrors the life path of my brother. He has loved skiing since he was a youngster, growing up skiing on the sometimes glorious Vermont snow, or, on other occasions, navigating teeth-chattering ice on mid-winter ski trails. Perhaps he is even a better person for having taken in stride the good and the bad in life, just as one does each time one steps off the ski lift and starts down the trail—the bumps, stinging cold, deep snow, glorious sun-filled days, shuddering ice, even falls that result in a helicopter ride to the hospital.

As the skier rides up the Mad River Glen single chair-lift and arrives at the summit for the first run on a below-zero day, one has a general inkling of what lies ahead. But once on the snow-covered trail, the run down can throw the skier perilously off balance with barely controlled turns on large patches of ice and rocks protruding through thin snow cover. Or it can be a glorious ride on fresh snow with sweeping turns, passing slow skiers, peeling off to ride through unbroken snow in the woods, and feeling the power of one's legs as they adjust to nuances of snow and terrain. Even with the inevitable miscalculations and snowy wipeouts on a steep slope, Phil takes what comes and makes the best of it. Kinda like life.

———

Postscript: My brother Phil died in August 2018 after this story was written. I will miss him in my life . . . and miss skiing with him in the fresh snow and curving trails on a run down the mountain at Mad River Glen.

NANCY REID

Zebra Crossing
Evening Vespers

I am a lover of words and ideas and metaphors—things that seem to be one thing but are really something more or different. I grew up in Maine and graduated from a liberal arts college where, in the early '70s, we marched, boycotted classes, questioned authority, and deconstructed structure in any way we could. These were formative days for me. I came to Vermont in the late '70s to raise sheep and live off the land. Our lifestyle choices were informed by *Mother Earth News*, the Nearings, Ken Kesey, and *Our Bodies Our Selves*. After I completed my farmer-girl period, my husband and I raised two children while teaching public elementary school—a calling and a career that threaded through all the chapters of my life. I then spent another decade as a single mother of two young children. This was a hard test, but I believe I passed it. I recently moved to Montpelier, Vermont, to reinvent myself as a single woman, mostly retired, living in town and discovering new adventures in writing, reading, socializing, and traveling.

Zebra Crossing

NANCY REID

We were quite a sight, trooping around the neighborhood. I am sure there were neighbors, unseen by us, peeking out from behind curtains.

Joining me were my two grandsons—Driscoll, age four, and Bailey, age two—and Amelie, my son's elderly but lovely rescue dog who was "temporarily" living with me. Being a grandmother (or Bibi as my grandboys call me) takes many forms. I had just picked the boys up at their day care and taken them to my house, and our first important job was to take Amelie out to "do her business." The boys had a little spat as to who gets to carry the poop bag, and I decided the best option was to have each boy carry his own bright blue biodegradable bag. Each boy was now poised and ready to do the scooping.

So there we were, parading around Dairy Lane and Terrace Street, Amelie at the other end of a retractable leash, the boys sporting blue poop bags, and Bibi trying to rein in the parade.

Needless to say, progress was slow. We needed to stop

for Amelie to sniff previous dog markings, for Driscoll to do a "nature pee," and of course younger brother needed to do the same. We met and greeted other dogs and dog walkers. With some effort, I kept the boys and bags, dogs and leashes from tangling.

Alas, the blue bags were not necessary. The boys couldn't grasp that you can't just command this act to happen, and so we headed home.

We came to the white zebra crossing that marks the intersection of Terrace Street and Walker Terrace, where I got the dog and boys to wait at attention on the sidewalk before proceeding. Driscoll is small—maybe thirty-five pounds—but on his own, he slowly stepped out into the road with hands outstretched, crossing-guard style, commanding the cars to stop. A black Jeep Cherokee and a large red Ford four-by-four construction vehicle—"RANDY'S ODD JOBS—NO JOB TOO SMALL—CALL 299-7850" painted on the side—slowed for the small boy with outstretched hands and the confidence that the vehicles would certainly stop. And they did. Once his authority had been established, his grandmother, younger brother, and leashed dog all crossed Terrace Street. Driscoll stayed halting the big vehicles until we were safely across, and we made sure to wave at both drivers. Randy (presumably) in the Ford truck needed to lean over the hood of his truck to see the small boy stopping traffic. I was struck by Driscoll's sense of authority—his confidence that the car and truck would stop and his sense of security and safety.

Safely across the road, I was reminded of another zebra crossing, this one in Nepal. A few weeks earlier, I had returned from Kathmandu, where I had spent a month volunteering at a local school. Each morning had I walked to school from my home-away-from-home. In Kathmandu, there is no order or structure to the traffic. I was told that the traffic lights had stopped working ten years earlier and hadn't been repaired. There were no stop signs and no working stoplights.

But there were faint zebra crossings. The problem was that drivers paid no attention to the markings. In order for young students to get to school, they needed to do this elaborate, carefully timed dart across the main street. I watched as a young girl—maybe six or seven and, like Driscoll, weighing about thirty-five pounds—in a crisp, clean school uniform and a Mickey Mouse backpack stood at the edge of the main road and looked one way, then the other way. Buses and trucks sped past, spewing fumes. The girl carefully watched the buses and construction trucks, gauged their speed, and then in a flash, dashed across the road. No vehicle slowed even a bit, but the girl with her bumping Mickey Mouse backpack was safely across the road and headed for school.

This was part of the morning routine—every morning, for every student—and they had become expert at the carefully timed dash across the road. Needless to say, the zebra markings were largely ignored, as they served no function. Children crossed at any random point on the road. I watched these children deftly and successfully cross the road every morning, and I marveled and I pondered. Their life was inherently unsafe and insecure. Trucks flew by, their drivers not seeing or caring about the children on the roadside. The children needed to rely on their own wits and skill, as there was no order around them. How did they define themselves in relation to the world with such constant and crushing disorder and danger?

I think of little Driscoll, with outstretched hands and a blue bag sticking out of his pocket, stopping the large truck for his grandmother, his dog, and his younger brother. He is growing up with a sense of his power and knowledge that the world—his world—is ordered and safe and he has the inner resources—the authority—to stop big trucks and the security to know that they will stop for him. I ponder the difference and what that difference portends for children growing up in very different parts of the world.

Evening Vespers

NANCY REID

We knew it was time for evening vespers when we saw mother's cigarette tip coming up the stairs—a torch to announce her arrival—small and bright in the dark. As soon as we saw this beacon, Gail scrambled from her bed, on the other side of the loft, to mine. She padded over, barefoot, and jumped under my covers. Our bedroom was the entire upstairs of a small cape. Her part was far larger than mine, but mine was a bit more private because it was separated from the rest by swinging doors. Gail and I pretended that they were saloon doors like the ones we saw on *Bonanza*. This was enough to make my bed the preferred one for evening stories. By the time my mother was at the top of the stairs and turning through the saloon doors, Gail was snuggled in with me, and we were waiting.

Like any religious service, Mother's stories were predictable, always the same. She sat on the end of my bed and started with a song—a Jesus song, even though we were not particularly observant Christians.

Jesus loves me! This I know,

For the Bible tell me so . . .

We sang together, the three of us, quietly and reverently. It was a very different tone than the one we had used while singing "What Will We Do with the Drunken Sailor" around the piano less than an hour before. This was more like a hymn or a lullaby. We got to the end of the song and proceeded to say a series of prayers. Together we first said:

Thank you God for a lovely day
For time to work and time to play
For pretty things my eyes to see
And people to love and who love me.

And then always:

"Oh God whose laws will never change, we thank thee for these things we know, that winter always brings the spring, that after rain the sun will shine, that life goes on and love remains and life and love will never end. Amen."

Then we blessed people and pets that were important to us, Gail and I each contributing names. The list of the blessed always included our younger brother, Bob, and grandparents and friends. This was the only part of the litany that might change—as friends, crushes on boys, and important events like birthday parties or summer camp came and went.

Once the personal blessings were done, Mother's turn was over. Never any hugs, kisses, or "Good night, dear"s. Her nightly gift to us was like an anthem—the prayers and songs that never change, in kind or sequence. We wanted it to be just like that, always exactly the same, solid and predictable, a ritual that we had memorized and could count on. She left, and up the stairs came my father, sans cigarette. (I wonder, fifty years later, did they pass each other on the stairs, share a greeting or a smile?)

As soon as my father started up the stairs, Gail and I

started twitching with excitement. The best part was coming up. We knew it. He came through the swinging doors and sat at the foot of my bed. Gail and I were huddled under my bedcovers, knees tucked up under our chests, at the ready. He always started the same way, without any introduction or greeting.

"Once upon a time there were two little…" Then there was a hush of suspense while he concocted a story. He had the brilliant ability to improvise a little tale right off the top of his head. He spun us a story, and it was invariably original, spontaneous, and outrageous. It could be "two little penguins" or maybe "two little anteaters" or even "two little canoes" but there were always two and they were always little.

The tale that unfolded was always about some bit of trouble these two little somethings got into and out of. The tales had plot, detail, climax, and closure and always ended happily. What we anticipated with such excitement was not so much the little story itself but rather the very moment right after "two little." The endless possibilities and the fact that he didn't know what the next words would be either, made this a delicious moment. Then once the moment was over and the characters were announced— or, rather, flopped out of his head—the story unfolded with magic, literary devices, and charm. We were captivated until the very end, and then he, too, returned down the stairs, again with no hugs or endearments. His nighttime blessing was the story of endless possibilities and unpredictability and dramatic anticipation. Then it was just us. Nighttime vespers were over, and we were graced with complementary gifts from our parents: from my mother, security, stability, and a well-worn love, and from my father the gift of surprise, a sense of unseen and unknown wonder just around the corner, and a dazzling and magic love. The balance was perfect.

Gail scurried through the saloon doors and back to her bed, blew a kiss over her shoulder, and whispered, "'Night, Nance."

"Good night, Gail," I answered tenderly.

NANCY TUCKER

Around the Kitchen Table
Keeping Up to Date

I'm a child of the 1950s. Like most families I knew, our dad went off to work each day and our mom stayed home and took care of the kids and the house. My three siblings and I grew up in the suburbs of Connecticut. Life was not fancy, but we had everything we needed, including a happy childhood.

I could not have predicted that my adult life would take a very different turn. I became a single mother by choice and raised my son on my own. We lived in an 1850s farmhouse on a back road in Vermont. I learned to split wood, thaw frozen pipes, and bail water from the basement during a flood. For thirty-four years I have juggled a variety of home-based businesses and part-time jobs to pay the bills. When things get stressful, which is nearly every day, I write in my journal. Writing helps me process my thoughts, sort out my emotions, and remember the details.

I am so grateful to now be part of a group of writing friends, sharing our stories and encouraging each other.

Around the Kitchen Table

NANCY TUCKER

L ike most families during the 1950s, ours gathered around the kitchen table for supper every night. It was not dinner, it was supper. Ours was always served right at 5:30, when Dad arrived home from work.

If we were transported back to that kitchen, with the fluorescent overhead light shining down on the scene and the six of us sitting around the white enamel-topped table, we would be appalled at how tiny the space now seems.

A single-basin sink with enamel drain boards on either side ran along one wall of the kitchen. Windows over the sink gave a view of the yard and driveway so Mom could keep an eye on us as we played.

The electric stove occupied the adjacent wall with two metal cabinets mounted above. Below the cabinets, on either side of the stove, were two tiny countertops not much bigger than cutting boards.

A narrow closet with shelves held the Lu-Ray dishware, Mom's collection of spices, and mixing bowls. On the floor of that closet Mom stored the potatoes and onions and the basket with the items that needed ironing.

When we gathered around the table for supper, I always sat between Mom and Dad. My two older sisters and our younger brother sat opposite us. Things were so tight that if someone needed an extra serving off the stove, Mom turned and reached it from her chair. If we needed something from the fridge, Dad had to stand up and move because his chair was smack against the fridge door.

Mom drew on recipes from her 1941 copy of *America's Cook Book* with the thick black canvas cover that proudly proclaims "This cover is washable." Perhaps that is the reason it has survived and is now on the shelf at my house.

Inside that cookbook are black-and-white photos of food preparation and recipes that are, quite frankly, very worrisome. I spot a recipe for "Chicken Mold" and "Frozen Prune Pudding" and "Fish Stuffed Cucumbers." Thankfully, none of these were ever served at our house. But I do recall most of the meals Mom served: spaghetti with meat sauce, chili con carne, fried chicken, meat loaf, macaroni and cheese, chopped suey, chicken pot pie, Swiss steak, hamburgers, hot dogs, and a thing called noodle casserole. Sometimes Mom would buy frozen fish sticks and a bag of French fries and then we had fish and chips with tartar sauce.

On rare occasions, Dad would bring home a single large pizza from John's Pizza down the street. It was a thin-crust pizza, dripping with olive oil on top. As Dad pulled slices from the pie, with strings of mozzarella dangling, and plopped those slices on our plates, my mouth would water with anticipation. I remember it as the best pizza I ever had.

On even more rare occasions Dad would go into town and come home with hamburgers and French fries from White Castle. They came individually wrapped in white bags with grilled onion and a slice of dill pickle on each burger. They were such a treat that sixty years later I can still remember the delicious, greasy smell of those hamburgers and fries and the delight of enjoying them together around that table.

On Sunday we had our main meal after church. Mom might roast a chicken or fry pork chops in a pan or broil a steak until it was well done and burnt around the edges. I had no idea it was okay to eat meat with red in the middle until I went away to college.

At our house no one served themselves. Your meat was portioned out and put on your plate. If there was extra food, second helpings were offered, but generally we didn't expect more than was put on our plates. We were fine with that plan.

Salads were another story. Mom made a great Jell-O salad with grated carrot and crushed pineapple. Even today, after all the jokes our generation makes about Jell-O salads, I would slurp that thing up if someone would bother to make it for me. It was cool, refreshing, and had a tiny bit of crunch from the carrots.

When Mom made tossed salad, that was iceberg lettuce with sliced carrots and one or two tomatoes cut into wedges. She made her own salad dressing this way: pour a little oil over the salad, pour a little red wine vinegar and then squirt ketchup over the salad greens and mix it up. Every once in a while, when no one is looking, I still use that combination on salads I serve because it's actually quite tasty, even if Martha Stewart would never suggest it.

A simple dessert came next. It might be canned fruit served with a homemade oatmeal cookie or a brownie. Ice cream was another frequent dessert offering. Sealtest was the brand Mom bought. At the time, a half-gallon container actually held a half-gallon of ice cream. Once in a while we had something fancy like store-bought éclairs.

These came in a package of five but because we were a family of six, Mom would not have an éclair. I remember feeling bad about that. We would take turns sharing bites of our treat with her. We were learning that when there isn't enough of something, or when something about the meal is imperfect, Mom makes the sacrifice.

After supper the table was cleared and the plates were stacked by the sink. They would be washed later by some combination of the three sisters. There was no dishwasher in the house until we were all teenagers.

With the meal out of the way, Mom arranged the kitchen table to make bag lunches for the next day. Out came the loaf of Wonder bread and the box of waxed paper. She quickly put together peanut butter–and-jelly, or cheese, or tuna, or meatloaf sandwiches. She wrapped each one in wax paper and put it into a brown bag with an apple or a banana and a paper napkin. When Mom occasionally bought deli meat for our sandwiches, it was always boiled ham. She would order a half-pound and managed to make sandwiches for six with that amount. Each sandwich had one slice of ham, one slice of Velveeta cheese, and a smear of French's yellow mustard. Mom was a child of the Depression. A single slice of meat was enough for a sandwich.

Our evening meals together around that kitchen table were part of the daily routine at our house. It was a time when we were asked about our day, our homework, and our friends. We teased each other and told jokes. My sisters would discuss cheerleading practice or the camping trip with the Girl Scouts. My brother and I would kick each other under the table and then deny it.

My siblings and I learned a lot of things sitting around that table as a family. We might not have learned about fine cuisine but we learned about being thrifty. We learned basic manners such as waiting for each other, cleaning our plates, listening to each other, and cleaning up our messes. We learned that our parents cared about us and wanted to hear what we had to say. That table became a symbol of our gathering in as a family. Eventually of course, we each left our seats at that table as college, jobs, and marriage pulled us away. But the memories of those times and the lessons learned there remain bright.

Keeping Up to Date

NANCY TUCKER

Here is my question of the week: When did wearing pants become passé?

Apparently I have not been paying attention. I work at a Vermont Welcome Center where visitors from all over the world stop by. Those of us working behind the desk see pretty much everything when it comes to fashion, from total grunge to Montreal chic.

When we spot a visitor wearing something unusual, my coworkers and I often look at each other and raise our eyebrows as if to signal "Well, that's different!" In recent years it has become common to see a woman wearing a top and tights without the benefit of a tunic or slacks to cover her derrière. The first few times I spotted this, I said to myself, "Excuse me, but isn't that woman walking around in her underwear?"

On a recent trip to the Dartmouth College campus I noticed first one young woman, then another, then another, wearing leggings rather than pants. They were all walking around town showing off their tushes. "Wow!" I shouted to myself. "When did this happen? And how could

I have not been noticing?" I'll bet that if I had a Y chromosome, I would have been noticing.

Apparently I'm more clueless than I realized. When I Google the question "When did women start wearing leggings instead of pants?" I discover this was being discussed on an Internet chat site in 2010. How could it be that six years ago people were discussing this fashion trend and I'm just now waking up to it?

A recent blog post by Vermont writer Anne Aikens addresses this same topic. In her article she asks, "When did pants become foolish? Our mothers didn't want us to wear pants in public; now our kids don't. Hell, we fought to wear pants. I'm wearing them." Me too. You won't spot me showing off my behind in tights or leggings anytime soon.

Here's another thing that I am apparently clueless about: Using checks to pay for items at stores. When did this become passé? I pay for things by check all the time. If I have a small purchase, say under twenty dollars, I will use cash, but otherwise I write a check.

I rarely use my credit card at a store. That's an old habit. Paying for things with a card has always felt like a big deal to me. The check register is my friend; it helps me keep track of things. I don't own a debit card. A dozen debit or credit card receipts floating around my purse would only add to the confusion of my life.

But a recent encounter at the supermarket startled me. The woman ahead of me in line was paying with a check. There was some sort of problem with the cash register accepting the check, and it took several minutes for things to get sorted out. The young woman in line behind me became annoyed. She commented aloud, "Debit cards have been around for years. Why doesn't everybody use them?" I proceeded to pull out my check to pay for my groceries and let her think about her remark.

The next week I took note of the picture on the cover of *Seven Days* newspaper. There was a cartoon of a caveman at the grocery store counter, writing a check for his purchases, and behind him in line was a young man fuming and making a face. "Oh, my God," I said to myself. " I'm that caveman and *Seven Days* is mocking me!"

I do worry that someday rather soon, like during my lifetime, checks may disappear and I will have to adjust to a debit-card lifestyle. I will not go there easily.

Oh, times do change and we have to adjust to those changing times. As a little girl my grandmother crossed the Kansas prairie in a covered wagon. Fifty years later, when she traveled to Kansas for her father's funeral, she went by airplane. And twenty years after that, she witnessed a man landing on the moon. My grandmother managed to adjust to a lot of new things during her lifetime.

I'll adjust to changing times too. Now that I've overcome my initial shock, I suppose it's not so terrible for young women to wear leggings instead of pants. I'm sure leggings are more comfortable than the thick wool slacks that my generation wore in winter.

And if other people want to swipe their debit card every time they pass through the checkout at the grocery store, that's fine, but I'm going to stand there and annoy you by writing a check for my purchase until the bank snatches that thing out of my hands.